THE ENEMIES OF LEISURE

THE
ENEMIES
OF
LEISURE

POEMS BY
JOHN GERY

Published by Story Line Press, Inc.
Three Oaks Farm
Brownsville, OR 97327

This publication was made possible thanks in part to the generous support of the Nicholas Roerich Museum, the Andrew W. Mellon Foundation, the National Endowment for the Arts and our individual contributors.

Cover Photo: David Brumbach, *Lancaster Train Station*, 1978. Reproduced by permission of Science Press, Ephrata, Pennsylvania, ©1992.

Book Design by Michele Thompson

Library of Congress Cataloging-in-Publication Data

Gery, John
The enemies of leisure: poems/ by John Gery
    p. cm.
ISBN 1-885266-01-4
I. Title.
PS3557.E745E54 1995
811'.54—dc20   95-14689
                                                     CIP

ACKNOWLEDGEMENTS

Acknowledgements are made to the editors of the following publications where some of these poems first appeared, sometimes in different versions. The author wishes to thank the editors for permission to republish the poems here:

Chariton Review: "Deep South"
Crosscurrents: "What Are Chores?" and "A Sleep and a Forgetting"
Cumberland Poetry Review: "The Shape of Sadness"
Descant: "Photograph from the Gulf Coast"
Die Young: "Anti-Hemingway"
Embers: "The Barracuda," "A Bad Performance But My Own," "On All These Ideas In America," and "On Moving, On Moving On"
Maple Leaf Rag: "The Homeless and Me"
Nebo: "Afterthought" and "Living with Max"
New Virginia Review: "American Ghost" and "What We Imagine"
North Dakota Quarterly: "Dark Horse"
Outerbridge: "For Sally Ann, Wherever She Is, In Alabama"
Piedmont Literary Review: "A Great Woolly Mammoth," "Love's Myriad Alterations," and "On the Other Hand"
Pig Iron: "The Game of the Week"
Poem: "Pandora's Gift" and "For the People of Lesbos"
Poetry Project Four: "Being and Tire"
Pteranodon: "The Last Wallenda"
River City: "To the Pedestrian Crossing Elysian Fields at Humanity in New Orleans"
South Dakota Review: "The Arbitrary Edge," "The Enemies of Leisure," "To a Friend's Wife," and "Death in Various Parts"
Southwest Review: "What It's Like to Travel Long Distance Alone on the Train"
Swallow's Tale: "The Fat Lady at the Liquor Store"
Verse: "Speech for a Possible Ending"
William and Mary Review: "The Impropriety of Trees"

"A Sleep and a Forgetting," "Pandora's Gift," and "Speech for a Possible Ending" have also been previously published as a limited edition chapbook, *Three Poems*, by Lestat Press, West Chester University, West Chester, PA, 1989. "A True Lie" and "On Moving, On Moving On" received the 1987 Deep South Writers Poetry Prize.

The author wishes to thank Barbara Eckstein, Maxine Cassin, and Dana Gioia for their invaluable advice and assistance in assembling this collection.

CONTENTS

IV

Happiness appears to depend on leisure.
—Aristotle

AMERICAN GHOST

Not quite so collapsible
as you may imagine, these bones
of the fundamental country,
they hold up loosely within
the spirit, the American ghost,

fit like an elegant shirt
around a clean, lapidary body
so you can see they are cut
from the same cloth, no things
without the ideas we call them by

when comes the time to bless
and eat: We ingest neatly
the white corn. We inhale
after that the air, and swallow-
ing whole hog what we have been

given, we stroll out into the open,
even if no one else notices us,
the field itself we are crossing
much like any other field, fallow
for yielding us its rich future

after a rest. And we are assured
by our very invisibility, pressed
deep into our flesh, of ourselves,
footloose and bravely unseen
yet thought of, all the same.

I

I confess
I love that
which caresses
me.
                —Sappho

FIRST MUSIC

Young women have bodies, too,
    young men tend to forget
        in their hurry to sell them

theirs: Susan Harbinger,
    pleasure princess of my
        fifteenth year, O where

has yours taken you?
    What odor has soured
        the fragrance of your

lunular lips and belly,
    those breasts protruding be-
        fore me up in the front

row of the high school
    concert band? Would that
        I were that silver flute

you so preciously handled
    those long hours, to have had
        your narrow fingers running

over me, your soft mouth on
    my embouchure playing
        Everything's Coming Up

Roses
    in a flat 4/4. Am
        I, sweet Lesbia, now so dis-

mantled from that first song,
   my various body sections
      kept warm by the felt inside

the leather case you hide
   in your hallway closet, to be
      occasionally kicked

by your dour husband
   home late again tonight
      from his bad job?

Or maybe
   your white cotton gloves
      are what I once was,

the evening you thought
   no one was watching you, out
      behind the bandshell lot

as you stroked yourself
   between your plaid woolen
      thighs. O would that I

might arise, a sparrow
   in your palm, a melody
      you believe in, even now.

LOVE'S MYRIAD ALTERATIONS

Fine. If that's how you like cocktail glasses
stacked, if tapioca pudding isn't
your idea of heaven, if precision
razor blades, Bach's fugues, and pure molasses
don't jive with your homespun middle class's
folderol, and Queen Anne chairs aren't christened
by your Midwest autarky, imprisoned
here with me, then why should we make asses

of ourselves? I'll pack. I'll play the remover.
I'll take my TV set, my Tylenol,
my coffee grinder, and the other odds
and ends of independent life, my oeuvre,
and rent another place, just down the hall,
take up the sextant, worship roving gods.

A GREAT WOOLLY MAMMOTH

frozen alive these last four long
days in my apartment, I have gone
unshaven, unbathed, all rapture un-
captured, stepping out only once
or twice for a newspaper, maybe
squaring the corners, maybe shearing
the heat asunder with the frost
on my breath, as I bungle into knowing
I am obsolete—the vast hulky brute
none can nor will mate with
some fifteen imaginary million years
later: "O where have you been?"
asks a vaguely female telephone
to which, nodding, unkindly I honk,
"I have forgot, you have forgot,"
my elongated, desultory trunk un-
veloping into a hairy groan, but
"Don't run." "Well, I've got to"
despite my "you'll see I mean no harm,"
my tusks a white drill thrust
into my solid wall, stuck a moment,
then gone, with a static hiss
from where I lumber over, wavering,
to the other side of my cell cold
block:
    Stone me, primitives! Stone me!
For I have been kept among those
sadly preserved in the ice, before
coming to you in my loneliness,
and shall return, once I have fed,
and shall return, as I have said,
newly shaven and smelling fresh
with a rock, a scissors, and the rest.

For Sally Ann, Wherever She Is, In Alabama

All good Americans are not, of course,
supposed to have *taste*. "I have even seen,"
says Mencken (p. 500), "*jonteel*, in a trade name,
for *gentil*, and *parfay* for *parfait*."
On my trade name television today I saw
like anyone else the detonated collapse
of the now gone once colonial Grand Hotel
in a silent Panasonic boom boom.

Which took me to parfaitly beootifool Sally,
her breasts blooming out of her antebellum
brood—enough to make anyone's jonquils grow.
And her white patch of forehead
and her tiny corked-up nostrils
and her arms and her hands that can't handle
grocery bags or Pontiac doorhandles well. Oh,
Sally Ann, soft Sally Ann,
                                        but what of your garden toes
squeezed though they are in your high-heeled
sabots? Why when you walk with those toes
pointing outward do I see my own baby
dropping out from between your knees
like a suddenly errant basketball,

your mouth tight as a drawstring, your tongue
severely tied back, like that time you reached
for another cigarette before continuing
our long conversation on Van Gawk?

THE FAT LADY AT THE LIQUOR STORE

It must be my airy thinness
that keeps from me the sweet *Hello*!
the others pluck from her cornu-
copia daily. I don't drink much,

am therefore mostly absent from her lair,
that corner where the hard stuff is shelved,
Early Times, Old Dickel, Old Grand Dad,
those Bourbon stalwarts blocked out

behind her blue-cotton, clean, size 97
labor dress, out-bowed around the waist,
her white plastic belt melted and stretched
no doubt to adapt to her summer globosity.

I admit it. I'm no Roman senator
greeting plebians with a hand toss
of my toga (under which, were she
curious, she'd discover indurate ribs)

since my brow is as stern as my sternum
prominent. Yet within her billowy breasts
and thighs, within her bulging cheeks, their
very mallowness, hides the mystery

of cabalistic calories and bones,
the knowledge of facing choices
and turning not one of them down,
like that truly republican daughter

Julia, of Augustus, who knew the wiles
of tens of thousands of lusty men.
At me she smiles, if I smile first;
I lose myself in the crowds, though,

the molecule I already am, and break
my brains on how to become more imposing.
She must know me at least to appear
as quaintly peculiar as she is

but we never speak to each other.
Back home playing with my supper peas,
I think of Horatius Flaccus, living
off the land, sending messages monthly

to Maecenas in Rome: "I am fine.
Plenty of Sabine wine here, good
food, too, so I've put on some weight,
am sometimes lonely for women."

THE GAME OF THE WEEK

Before the bottom
  half of the fifth
    we began to undress

each other and Joe
  Garagiola said,
    Now here's a gentle-

man both on and off
  the field. Was I
    ever impressed?

Well, yes—once—
  when I thought
    I heard a low

and outside curve
  nip the corner.
    We both looked

up and I knew then
  that love is nothing
    more

than the right
  collusion of
    shared discipline

and pitching signs,
  and had you not been
    already there, I

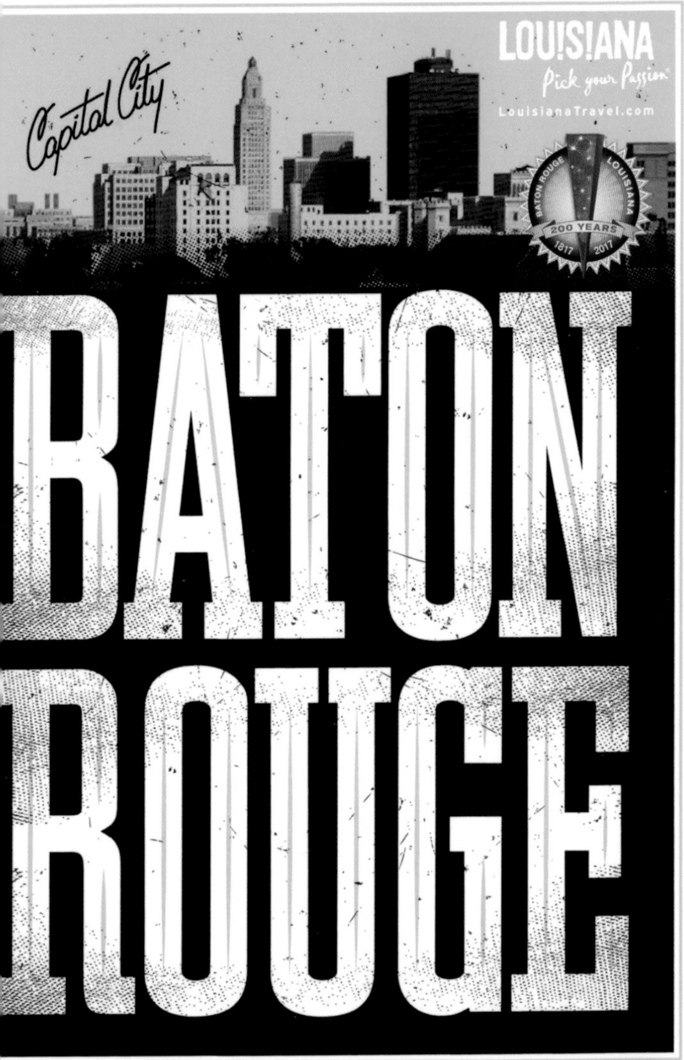
Capital City
LOUISIANA
Pick your Passion
LouisianaTravel.com
BATON ROUGE
LOUISIANA
200 YEARS
1817
2017
BATON
ROUGE

Visit Baton Rouge

www.batonrouge200.com
"Capital City" by Jonathan Palmisano

U.S. POSTAGE ≫ PITNEY BOWES

ZIP 70806
02 4W
0000351388

$ 000.34⁰

would have greeted
   you and kissed you,
       as I would again

now, with talk
   about
       the standings.

PHOTOGRAPH FROM THE GULF COAST

Five feet away that fat man stood from us,
on our last crossing to the coast, and caught
these smiles, my arm around you, and the bus
we had just stepped from, on which we had fought

for hours, though what about I've since forgotten,
as usually I did the moment after
despite the acrid taste of something rotten,
the smell of silences, the dearth of laughter.

What I do remember now, thinking of it,
is how your nose was angled toward the glass
crosswise, so I would have to look above it,
yet not aslant enough for you, alas,

to look at me, my trapped and angry stare
attesting dully to your bated soul,
our mutual display of so much care
it lacked concern. That willing tourist's role

was to record our bodies, decked and shored,
whose faces here survive his double chin—
my frozen eyes, glazed over, vague and bored,
your rigid mouth constricted to a grin—

yet gave him, casting idly on the sand,
a passing reason to be passing there,
to take a picture, innocent and bland,
of two hearts drowning in the open air.

THE BARRACUDA

What was that fish we came on, at the last,
snorkeling above the reefs off Water Isle?
Suddenly in my field of view, it flashed
like sunlight off a plane's windshield a mile

or so away, intense enough to burn
the surface of my retina, but brief,
too brief to wreak much damage. With a turn
and twist, it disappeared behind the reef

to feed on lichen, leaving me to wonder
if I had just imagined it, or if,
a moment later, it might drag me under.
I flapped to signal you, but you were stiff:

Had you not seen it, too preoccupied
by angelfish that poked around the coral
to glimpse, beyond their blue, its silver glide
whose progress like a story without a moral

might suffer us its ending only once—
a simple, painful death, one thrashing bite
separating us for good? My hunch,
admittedly unproven in the light

of our no longer traveling together,
is that it was a barracuda, yet
because it sensed the danger in the weather
it fled, not like a sinner from regret

nor even less like listeners from a reading
where every poem rambles on or rhymes,
but like a driver ticketed for speeding
leaving the scene of once and future crimes

who knows from past experience it's wise
to slide out quietly, then to withdraw.
If only we had come to recognize
the barracuda neither of us saw.

DEEP SOUTH

They are used to it
so on their front stoops
they sit daily, from late

morning like the caged
squirrel monkeys drugged
silently at the zoo

until well after dusk has
obscured the cloying sun, wet
from their lemonade or

the Mississippi dew they
absorb all day long, while way
upriver lurking longshoremen

gruffly wipe the white sweat
from the backs of their black
necks and just swear

nothing they know could be
more like the bitter
fires of hell than this

unloading of flatboats
in August, though I know
better because I have

struggled with the words
that would make you peel
off your yellow sundress in

my presence, then feel
the stress of my desire
inside you without

my doing anything more
than the starting in,
as the clear red molds of

sweat on your shoulders
bead there, betraying
your mild submission, no

matter that we just
go on with it, blindly
unmindful, like our

other neighbors, the rich,
who have everything,
everything done for them

by relative strangers,
who keep cool by moving
the spaces around them

with numinous dollars, who
never bother to stop in
the middle of things

to consider, oh, how we
might ever over-
come our sad plight and

in this heat might learn
to get used to things, to
anticipate feeding time

or otherwise scramble
for visitors only, their
admiring glances, so

to worship not each
other but the midday sun,
what it might teach us

before going down, or
the nights here, which
   ometimes are tender.

TO A FRIEND'S WIFE

There is a pain so delicate
we consider it luxurious
to suffer—walking into
a spiderweb across an eyelid
or catching the tiny chaff
of broken bits of eggshell
in the throat. To you,
dear friend, I owe this pain.

Such a pleasure it is to sit
with you by my shoulder
when mildly I can tell,
though your clear gaze is hid
as we page through your photographs
and in my voice I feign
a calm, that we are a spurious
pair, who can say nothing bolder
than we are not alone,
we are not alone.

A BAD PERFORMANCE BUT MY OWN

I never saw
The Heavens so dim by day. A savage clamor!
Well may I get aboard. This is the chase;
I am gone forever.

[Exit, pursued by a bear.]
—Antigonous in *The Winter's Tale*

Today I have discovered nothing
new, yet you continue to rage
against that part of me unchanged
and still unacceptable to children,
who, were they themselves anyway,
would probably grow up to become
princesses or roving musicians
crawling all over northern Bohemia,

so I am taking no further chances
and will admit how elusive I've been,
like water in a dried-up riverbed
atop a cold mountain of boulders, love
the emotion you point out I choose
to dance by until I evaporate and
lo, I am afraid—
surprise and life at that moment

my excuse, a mere supporting male
in our contract: I live to take
orders, not to make anyone happy
but to carry upstream a sperm,
advise a queen, or two, deliver
unwanted infants by the strange raw
sacks in which they are planted
during the season before the rains

swell up suddenly and we all sink
deep below the sodden surface
of our hardrock skin, to preserve,
if not the infants themselves, then
the stories they would have us tell
them. This is no easy task and today
I have discovered nothing more
about how otherwise to pursue it

yet you continue to growl at
that part of me I cannot escape,
my own order—you who yourself are
full of surprises, harboring what
virtues you engulf in the very fur
you smother your bony victims with,
sagebrush rolling over the boulders,
and I, who am angry too, should act

things out, not settle for compromise,
as Antigonous does, but bluntly defy
the cagier elements, follow a master's
voice more blustery than the storm,
spare the infants' lives, yes, put to
one side, but when the ship goes down,
insist how stage directions can lie,
even in comedies, and, casually, die.

II

To work and suffer is to be at home.
All else is scenery.

—Adrienne Rich

ON MOVING, ON MOVING ON

for Barbara

It isn't the outside that matters
but the inside. I have seen them,
insides, after bothering too long
with each minute square of the street
and the carefully ordered cornices
here, there, across the alleyways,
as though I, staff in hand, could reveal
violently the life behind the veneer
by starting with the veneer. Who
knows? Maybe we can only enter
from the outside thousands of times
before we realize that it was inside
where we, in fact, began and should
remain, even in the sunniest weather.

That's why talking with you today
I broke into a fine sweat, its thin fissure
appearing along my hairline, wider
on the inside than you might imagine,
a surefire crack, a last buffalo
giving vent to its strange wild rage
as close to invisibility as carnally
possible. Who knows? The trees
lining the street hide most of their
tell-tale rings, I hide my bold looks,
the rooms behind their closed shutters
and drawn shades fading like stars
expose their past even while consuming it,
and most of the classics are obscure

to all but a chosen few, just as they,
turning over the final page, feel inside
the hot steam rising from cement after rain
and think it peculiar, like old garlic
returning to the spleen to settle down
after a handsome meal, that we others,
seeming Jesuits, are starving for the taste
of what we have been taught to call the good
in life—a comfortable room, an empty mind
of one's own, the pretty aroma alone there
as the eternally disappearing sign: These,
and that yet even finer distinction
between private ownership and the love
of a happy intruder, have been known to me

before now and will, with the sudden drop
of any hat and coat on my soon proven-to-be
new doorstep, be inadvertently redefined
by their not being evident. Who knows?
Look at the stoop. And as you sit, thrilling
to the secret hype of the sycamore trees'
intoxicating glue, imagine staying on awhile
outside, without the benefit of ceremony,
like crossing the range without a wagon,
and you, too, will snap at the story
only the neighbors can tell, of the fast,
fast lives they have spent here, once
they no longer overlook you and can see you
as not so young as not really to matter.

LIVING WITH MAX

To be a cat at our house wasn't fun,
although the boy who hated cutting the grass
and thought a boy's few chores were never done
would think so, waiting for those days to pass

until he was old enough to quit that lawn—
its summer weeds, its piles of leaves in fall,
its winter ice he'd scatter cinders on—
and like an escaping convict scale that wall

beyond the rose bushes, thorns, and vines to creep
among the world's fields for the milk, field mice,
and moon he thought they held. But boys will leap
to rash conclusions. Our cats, however nice

it may have been to stalk the premises
outside our house by night or rub their backs
by day against our legs, one nemesis
from birth had learned to live in fear of: Max,

the tyrant watchdog, who despised all creatures
he sensed might fit between his jaws—cats, birds,
squirrels, chickens, ducks, the milkman's foot, the preacher's
divining hand—and never could mere words,

although we exercised whole lexicons
of curses and commands, control the terror
Max would, unleashed, unleash on his feline pawns,
who as his pages, jester, and crownbearer

lived in peril, knowing any second
might spell their doom; they never could be sure.
That boy, until he grew up, never reckoned
what cats, just as we all must, must endure.

THE ARBITRARY EDGE

We were much too hard on ourselves those days.
Of course, for some of us it was the sin
that did us in—girls fingered on doorsteps,
Jack Daniels, basements yellow with our smoke.
But for others just raking leaves was enough,
one fall, to crack us, or the incessant driving
from the high school lot to the root beer place,
George, Brian, Richard, Charles, Paul and I,
back and forth, back and forth, back and forth,
waiting for the jack rabbit under our skin
to shrivel, die, and make us a good luck charm.
Who after three long adolescent summers
of stealing peaches from his neighbor's grove
could happily sell health insurance
as Brian does, and Charlie, who was older,
planned to, before he left for Vietnam?

At fourteen I dreamt of the Viet Cong—
a handful of guerillas, surrounding
our house, each hidden behind a hedge or bush
my father had just clipped that day,
their Russian-built machine guns peeking out
from the forsythias and boxwood. Why,
I wondered, had they no knapsacks, no food,
no radios, no family, no way
of feeling as at home as I did there
where I knew every tree by name. They crouched
and when I peered down at them from my bedroom
they fired in quick bursts. I jerked awake.

                                  Next day
our neighbor, who worked the stockyards shoving
fat steer down a steel chute to their slaughter,
in neat rows mowed his lawn up to our yard's
line, then stopped. I stood and watched and waited
as he approached that arbitrary edge
between us, back and forth, back and forth.
Sixteen years later, last month I was told
how coming home one night from Neffsville, drunk,
he drove his old gray Buick over the edge
and into our Dutch elm. Yet think of us,
how fortunate we are to be alive,
too young for the last war, too old for the next.

THE LAST WALLENDA

That afternoon in Philadelphia
between the games of a doubleheader, rain
was threatening, as boys in baseball caps
ran off from their fathers, gathered near us
and dared decry the name *Wallenda*, dared
as he maneuvered his aging, clownish body
in mid-air, there above the stadium,
to mock him. We, who'd laughed through *Zarathustra*
and scorned all public acts, looked on unmoved,
while my friend Roy delivered several wry
remarks on children's viciousness in crowds.
With a horizontal rod pulled to his waist
creating gravity among the clouds
Wallenda held his weight in place and moved
by pointing toes outward so the arches
in his feet engulfed, unsteady as it was,
the tightrope—stretched from right field to left field.
It looked as though he wore my bedroom slippers.
Something as hard and old in those loud boys
as the appendix in the history of the body
wished Wallenda dead, with the hope that now
would come, like others' in his family,
his time to fall: How much more memorable
would be that day in Philadelphia
had Karl Wallenda dropped onto the infield
before the second game got under way.

Yet something else—I only think this now
since Roy and I no longer correspond,
he because he found me artificial
and I because, simply, he was too wry,
and since Wallenda died, finally, falling
as was said he would, one March in Puerto Rico—
something else as old as the appendix
prompts us to applause more than politely

when we watch a great ropewalker walking.
We're betting that his dare survives our dare,
that he will live in spite of those of us
who want him dead because he's supposed to die.
What does it mean to take a risk? I've known
the desire for death, or worse, for others' deaths
(though it isn't easy to admit that here),
not from a pathological fever,
of course, nor from a violent disregard
for humankind, or matter, or the heart.
But only for death's hardness and its sleep.

Wallenda dropped. And down with him, I'd add,
American Romanticism went
and Emigration to the West. We knew
from all our books, just as appendices
must be removed when undigested dross
clogs up the passages, the time would come
for life-and-death dares to exhaust themselves.
Indeed, we willed it, Roy and I, not just
by acting suave in Philadelphia
but by the way our whole friendship dissolved.
The tragedy of failing at a risk
is keeping distant from it afterwards,
remaining formal at all costs, and then
remembering how much you felt, or could
have felt, had you not been restrained. The Great
Wallenda, while he was alive, preserved
the possibility of tragedy,
but think of him, now that he's dead, as dead.
He failed, and proved our dare. So much for that.
If he were not a symbol of the grand
for vicious boys, we'd probably not think
here was a man who walked to make a living;
I wonder if we'd think of him at all.

WHAT WE IMAGINE

The distance of sound seems shorter
than the distance of silence—
so easy over the short waves
to hear the bleeding Arab girl
cry on her dead husband's body,
so hard to imagine the rest
of her life, the long afternoons
withering the desert on her skin, shots
no longer ringing, except in her ears,
while the other men she would have
circle softly like wolves around a carcass
too long abandoned, too long unclean.
Yet a smell carries better, they say,
in quiet air, and what we imagine
in the end is ours, day after dry day,
whether we offer it shelter or not,
harboring in us like a phrase
we thought we overheard someone say,
never knowing quite what it meant—
do something about it   just do
something   —hardly worth repeating
but as putrid as a bullet wound,
nearly as soundless.

INVASION OF THE SMALL MUSES

Across the street, behind a fence, the calls
of the little children at the daycare center
ensconce the air encircling my walls
(well, windows, really) through which would enter

under normal circumstances my views,
unvariegated by the fall, which can't.
So whose to blame, I wonder, for this ruse
depriving me my ordinary rant

against the state and season? Surely not
these children's parents, those overwrought chauffeurs
who've dropped them here in some mad bourgeois plot
to sic all offspring on the arbiters,

like me, of sense and reason—if not taste—
on us who, unlike them, childless and free,
determine to retrieve from our hours of waste
long testaments to lost democracy.

Nor presidents and bankers who, it's fair
to speculate, increasingly demand
that children's cries not heard be left to air
in order to insure their futures and—

what else?—their heirs enough to live on. No,
not they, but I, grown older and contrite,
who lean against my panes to watch them go
about their play. Yet squinting for the sight

of them flashing behind the fence, I cover
my ears, my nose pressed to the glass, and wince
insensibly, while all around me hover
small voices, sweet halloos and secret glints.

AFTERTHOUGHT

Only under the heavy eaves of evening
do I, having sweated on the daily fields,
bother to look out into the tired sky,
as it sighs, exhausted with its birds.
A few clouds, late on the horizon, sag
like spent lungs, giving into the sun's
rapid decline, and the air itself
seems lost, looking for a place to hide.
I always drift up, as the light empties,
backward to the sun's accomplishment,
as though, a biochemist, it could cure
this pestiferous disease of human progress
while under these eaves impatiently I wait
for its nepenthean release. It grays,
a little red behind the haze. Its sadness
couples with the first night breeze.
The moon, appearing like a sudden bruise,
keeps the sky from sleep, and restless
now, wishing I had found some new excuse
to go out into the darkness, I turn
from the west, head for the land of dreams.

FOR THE PEOPLE OF LESBOS

Mark my words, my dears, for the time that yields them,
now approaching, soon to withdraw to leave you
dust as blank as the eyes in your marble statues:
    I can restore you,

loved ones. Children, gather your elfish calves, your
knees that need my hands to express their gestures.
Faces cry before me but pretty faces
    give me their sorrow,

soak my parting dress with their tears. I want you
twice to come to me through the night—at first, be-
fore we're free to look at each other, touching
    nothing but shoulders,

back, and forehead; secondly, after dawn, my
promise, I shall put on your slippers, whisper
songs from Sappho, quietly leave you, who have
    twice brought me comfort,

comfort. Words are lost and we broke a statute,
delicately ruining love in this age.
Quick, though! Stay awake! As the sun is rising,
    I have another

time to give you back, and I want and yearn to
tell you, twice to tell you, that you are not dark,
not a fray of shadow—(but I have written
    now for your future).

III

But most of all, as summer slanted to an end, he was learning to love idleness, idleness no longer as stretches of freedom reclaimed by stealth here and there from involuntary labor, surreptitious thefts to be enjoyed sitting on his heels before a flowerbed with a fork dangling from his fingers, but as a yielding up of himself to time, to a time flowing slowly like oil from horizon to horizon over the face of the world, washing over his body, circulating in his armpits and his groin, stirring his eyelids.
—J.M. Coetzee

A Sleep And A Forgetting

Our birth is but the sleep and the forgetting,
though sleep takes up the greater time and bathing
occasionally breaks up this pattern
of sleep, forgetting, sleep, forgetting, sleep,
whenever you slap water on your cheeks
and your dead skin sloughs off into the sewers.

It's not a bad life, really, one of setting
a schedule, then of sticking to it, only
remembering exceptions, as does the housecat
who always takes her meals without emotion
ever since that time you failed to feed her
for no apparent reason. Otherwise

that I've forgotten how it feels to love you
(those letters I found recently and read
again as crisp as slick dry skin on a pillow)
has kept me up nights, this past week or two,
in darkness—with no apparent tears to keep
your memory from fading into sleep.

THE ENEMIES OF LEISURE

for JEC

At Jackson Square last Saturday at noon
the enemies of leisure sat down on a park bench
to plot their strategy against my turgescent idleness.
One of them, the one with green skin whose veins bulge
around his eyes, reached forward and down to pick up
pieces of stale bread I'd left for the pigeons
and the wood on the bench warped under the sweating thighs
of the rest of the enemies of leisure. I heard a butterfly
crying, or was it a disfigured moth? Another one,
the enemy of leisure with the red scrubbed hands,
lifted lint from the overcoat of a nearby sleeping vagrant
as I gathered in my newspapers and started to rise, and
sweeping the sidewalks with his yellowed eyes
the one with pimples called out. "Almost Sunday," he cried.

They know much better the label to put on a pretty day
than I do, the enemies of leisure. They work at it.
I am a small miracle and I know nothing.
I have nothing to do—but to some I am a giant
and last night the enemies of leisure, all seven of them,
marched in single file up the side of my bedpost, over
my feet, and across my legs, leaving tracks of purpose
deep in my blankets, burning the hair on my chest in their wake,
then chopping back my sideburns to bury land mines
under my temples. Today I tried memorizing Whitman,
"I lean and loafe at my ease, etc." and "as to you Death,
your bitter hug of mortality, it is idle to try to alarm me"
and so on but it was no defense and I am fading, I am fading.
The black-caped leader of the enemies of leisure scaled
my green schefflera to direct his attack from its leaves.
Like Tu Fu I drank wine from a white cup but it's no go.

I am losing my fortitude, I am asking you to visit me,
the enemies of leisure are shoveling the dust out
from underneath my slippers, the one in the brown 3-piece suit
is crawling up my arm now, making small entries on a clipboard,
his pencil is sharpened, his eraser has never been used.
His prognosis is grim. I repeat, I am dying, S.O.S.,
come to me quickly, you're my only chance, I will save for you
the tracks of purpose and the warm wine. Abandoning ship.
This may be the last letter you receive from me
that has no point to it.

TO THE PEDESTRIAN CROSSING ELYSIAN FIELDS AT HUMANITY IN NEW ORLEANS

Okay, so you believe the line
between us, painted white by some
white city worker years ago,
now fading, will protect you. Fine.
But I may not be quite as dumb,
packed in my Plymouth Alamo,

both windows rolled up tight as oyster
shells when they're plucked from ice and slapped
atop a table, as I look—
the spots under my armpits moister
than yours, my slender fingers wrapped
around the wheel as around a book,

the two dark circles of my glasses
enormous craters on the moon.
As you step from the curb, behind
your silhouette a storm amasses,
which happens every afternoon
when summer afternoons are kind,

so barely swerving to avoid
your black liquescent body, I
zip by you, then I lift my hand
to let you know how I've enjoyed
our brief encounter, the vague gray sky
drawing closer to the asphalt land,

but in my rearview mirror you,
in practicing your sullen craft,
feign nothing, though I glimpse a smile
falling to the avenue
where crossing it you might have laughed,
did laughter not show lack of guile.

BEING AND TIRE

*Dasein is always ambiguously "there"—
that is to say, in that public disclosedness of
Being-with-one-another where the loudest idle
talk and the most ingenious curiosity keep "Things
moving," where, in an everyday manner, every-
thing (and at bottom nothing) is happening.*

—Heidegger

How will they remember me,
these boys with their baseball bat
watching me across the street
change my tire? That little fat

one in red stripes, his round mouth
open wide, is so precisely
vacant I could be TV
or a northern snowstorm nicely

rolled into a snowman, for
all his peanut eyes can tell
at this distance, just too far
for him or his pals to yell

over to. I raise my hand
but I'm not of their kind, spirits
from some curious netherland,
one which draws me here to hear its

echoes: the gangly, overgrown
punk in tattered dungarees
talking wildly, his clone
bent and picking from his knees

scabs concealed beneath fresh dirt,
and the midget wearing glasses
too big for him—nothing, at
bottom nothing moving, passes

these boys by, not me, nor snow,
nor what matters in this world.
My tire changed, they'll let me go
back to my existence, hurled.

ON THE OTHER HAND

My left hand is no lover of my right
but rather like an unattractive wife
it hangs there, while this other tries to write,
turning nothing to something, death to life.
It's idle, evil even, just for spite,
the one who earns full union pay for trif-
les, dangling cigarettes and getting tight
or playing passive fork to my right's knife.

Unfortunately, I can't let it go
or feed it less or send it off to school
to learn the things my right hand doesn't know.
So damned accommodating, like a mule
wherever my right traverses it's in tow,
obedient and loyal as a fool,
a mirror to this other left to show
the right that always being right is cruel.

"WHAT ARE CHORES?"

you asked me once, "Why is my time like this?
So many chores to do I won't live long
enough." What's joy? I ask. Suspended bliss?
Like listening to this suspended song,
engaging its time simply for its time?
Going somewhere, somewhere you don't belong,
and staying until it's someplace? The sublime,
according to Longinus, crawls along

like ivy up a wall—wild, disciplined
and modest, showing nothing of its parts
to other than strangers, as though the wind
which rustles through its leaves in fits and starts
fit casually into its bland disguise.
Were blandness, though, a virtue in the arts,
we wouldn't tire so easily, our eyes
would linger, ears listen for silence, hearts

slow to the pauses in a poem's rhythm.
Our chores would seem the world's epitome
of timelessness, and idleness joined with them,
the Beast with Beauty sitting down to tea:
He speaking of the magic of his lands,
his moats, his mirrors, and his rings, while she,
dispensing teacups with her delicate hands,
learns slowly how their regularity

of labor (hers, in planning her escape)
and leisure (his, in pressing her to yield)—
her simple dress, his long black flowing cape—
all meeting here twice daily have concealed
the darker terror underneath, the loss
surrounding them, the forest and the field
just beyond his gates which neither can cross
unharmed, and in their sanctuary sealed

from time by time they spend their time together.
Like you, asking your question off the cuff,
as though it were a comment on the weather.
Or my reply, "We don't live long enough,
it's true," as we miraculously share
the same brief ennui, no way left to bluff
ourselves with our illusions of what's there,
no extracting diamonds from this rough.

for my mother

WAFFLE DAYS

I haven't had a waffle
for awhile—the kind that comes
from a waffle iron. *Why?*
I ask myself. The cross-stitch
design, rounded along the edge:
What a piece of work in batter!
A triumph of reason and kitch-
en love! A map, a maze
for the syrup and the awful.

Nothing seems to matter
anymore. Not breakfast.
Not books. Not empty beds.
To think it does is a lie.
But to think of waffles numbs
the heart, and vaguely, like lust,
I hunger for the waffle days.

A DUTY TO DEJECTION

How unlike me this odd and gangly humor, this awkward
teenager galavanting through long hot summer streets
until well after midnight! Out here on the edge of things
behind my picket fence and neatly attentive petunias
I wait to be justified by the long hand of the law
of sadness, arriving in a flash of light, hoarse voices
from headquarters downtown, on radio waves to no one,
piercing the darkness.
                              So many off-days it's been
since I've tossed a handful of gravel
at those shady windows banking the boulevard
of the consciousness that I can't even shrug anymore
without wincing. Instead, I climb down from my porch
to hide from the neighbors, rummage through my black rooms,
strap on the irons of melancholy. And it pays!

Since nothing is clear at this point why joke about it
unless with one you hardly know on your arm, your heads
thrown back like a pair of fish too small to make
good eating, you wander into the evening, swimmingly,
dashing as Fred Astaire, and trace shadows
with the magic hand of chance? Nowadays life is just
not funny. And you have your own reputation to protect
from those cavilers telling you you have had no meaning,
not since the beginning. The rest is a shame, a crime.
Yet so long as the world doesn't end, somebody has to
live like this, and it's a job you can depend on.

DARK HORSE

Behind those others
   I am running

for president. Don't act
   so surprised, look

at the holstein, white
   on black, covering

the round, rolling farms
   of Pennsylvania every

spring and summer, look
   up at their teats or in-

to their soft bellies
   where their calves, their

hard hooves ready, un-
   curl themselves

for that great leap
   forward. I am there:

the population tapping
   maple sap in New

Hampshire, the eucalyptus
   bark, the longest ear

of corn in Clinton County,
   sweet peas and soy beans,

bluefish and barnacles,
    I am that clean aroma,

that cool magenta sky
    in Wyoming, the canyon,

the everglade, the nation
    at large. Listen to me,

listen and look, look,
    a Pegasus kissing babies.

Pandora's Gift

Had it not been so complicated, say,
had she discovered not the things
she did—that snake's rattle, that ass's bray,
those needles for mosquito stings—
but normal things less likely to betray

a woman's curiosity—a bell,
for instance, or several bells that chimed
distractingly, disposing her as well,
or cowbirds' eggs, two lines that rhymed,
the noisy colors of an asphodel—

would she have learned that she was better off
being where not being there
made little difference? Or would she've scoffed
at having found her small box bare
of anything impeccably unsoft

(the music, say, of some third-rate composer,
exquisite, gentle, but not grand),
and so instead of damning him who chose her,
poor Epimetheus, had damned the bland,
inconsequential sins—as they arose there

in half-flight from the floor, like unswept dust—
of Epimetheus's gods,
those giants whose hearts, worn out and gone to rust,
prevailed by making up the odds,
by lasting long enough to outlast lust

like love? And what of us, if from the first
our evil had been ordinary,
our songs not beautiful, our hearts not cursed?
What good to be not bad but wary,
our only hope in hoping for the worst?

IV

Our passing is a facade.
But our understanding of it is justified.
—John Ashbery

A True Lie

To want to speak the truth is to trip
ever so tantivy over the exposed root
of some ancient tree, protecting you
from the steady flow of rain, its leaves
like the feathers of a guardian angel
or Mother Goose (in another tradition)
spread neatly over your overheated head
without your having the slightest idea
of heaven, your body dropping to the ground
at the speed of a freight train through a vacuum.
Water-flecked, the tree embraces you
with its glaze. You shiver underneath it
on your way down, and no one runs in
to save you nor to attend to your sores.
Really, though, it's not such a reprehensible
circumstance, depending where you
finally end up. Even the rain will stop
at some point, and you could come to regret
never having gone out walking in the first place.
Besides, we all need exercise or we'll get fat,
luxuriating in this false stillness of silence.

ANTI-HEMINGWAY

I have a lot of things to say but am not so tough
about getting to the point the moment you expect
a surprise. Just look at those untied U.S. senators,
for instance, bobbing like a bevy of pecksniffian hens
on a farm no cleaner than one you're liable to run into
during any drive to the country. Sure, they are rife
with scenic rhetoric for the weathercocks back home
but in the stalls of their business they take forever
to lay an egg. Some of us, it seems, have to wander
phrenologically over the bumps of confusion before we arrive
sweaty and exhausted but happy at last to find the place
we marked on the map. And then there are always
the introductions, awkward adjustments to the unknown,
squelching the desire to turn back, smelling the barnyard.
Yet while someone else is using the bathroom, the view,
which has nothing to do with our being here,
if you really must know, but which bears mentioning,
is as suddenly lovely and fresh as a young friend
who bursts into your favorite room with good news
so long awaited, impatiently, that your sigh
can practically be seen through the syllables
like (sigh!) this, with that moderate gush of fondness
men cherish as much as women do, that seamless implicity,
thus the graceful unwinding of things I wish for you
like dying at an advanced age of "natural causes,"
or my saying, "Excuse me while I think of the right word.
May I offer you something to drink in the meantime?"

ON ALL THESE IDEAS IN AMERICA

Ideas, like cattle, tend to run in such unruly herds
and often so resemble one another you can't give
proper names to any of them, nor choose favorites.
Not surprising, then, our fear of butchers
who admire our flanks and discuss our fresh cuts,
"I'd love to sink my teeth into that one," muttering,
or, "Might you rehash this one the Argentine way?"

And not unlike those cowboys of whom we are
so proud, sweeping stupidly across fenceless plains,
we stampede ourselves through cold mountain streams
and over the open fields of suspense and possibility
directly to our slaughter,
                              only the lucky stray
or the one willing to lie down with the dogs
escaping westward, temporarily, while the rest of us,
corralled forever in some north, are packaged
in the tight-lipped plastic wrap better suited
to the public well-being, to be ground down
finally to the ashes from which we sprang. Of course

our long and lonely journey is not so lonely
as it is long, since those around us are like us,
nothing, and being nothing, an expense
of spirit, a waste of shame, not even the coyotes
scavenging our thin remains, one brief, juicy meal
for idle minds in the cities, truly the unheard-of.

The Impropriety Of Trees

for MDG

Resist the impropriety of trees
you say—which rise haphazardly through the air
from where their gentle father, some kind breeze,
once dropped them, from where they had to tear

through roots, through earth, through heavy weeds, to stretch
odd limbs. A simple order, friend—you say—
the story with a human sigh, will fetch
the fullest understanding and display,

a weather we can all converse about
with strangers just as well as intimates.
Storm clouds may threaten us, strong winds may flout
the way we occupy ourselves with bits

and pieces of emotion, such as love
and other overrated miseries,
but avert that chaos you've been thinking of.
Resist the impropriety of trees.

Still, Dana, even as you urge, you wonder
if my incompetence, not unlike yours,
is as much a consolation as a blunder.
Each gnarled branch which first, it seems, obscures

later unravels naturally on
the same dense sun we tend to with such ardor
and bend to as our god. I'm sent and drawn
by arbitrary aching toward the border

of sense and nonsense, where the smallest leaf
might doubt its own uncurling as it grows,
where stories of our complicated grief
can suddenly unfold, like the repose

after the storm, refreshed yet commonplace,
yet still a trace unshaken by the breeze
that brought about this quartz contentment, grace
enshrouded by proprietary trees.

THE HOMELESS AND ME

As the homeless collect around the brisk fire
crackling in my stomach, assuming it better
than to curl up next to its reassuring sparks
to stand by the barrel, awake, palms turned down
in a gesture neither defiant nor entirely
open-ended out in this cold night, they
no doubt wonder at their own attraction
to my diverting body smell, relative to theirs
not without its pleasant dimensions, like snow
promising a school holiday despite the bitter
aspects of frostbite, starvation, the flu.
Nor do they say much, candidly, to each other,
all eyes gathered on what may become their source
of a temporary coup de théâtre, frankly ignored
for its potential as a guiding social force.

Together they sway back and forth. They poke
sticks into the crisp coals which, flaring up
like good ideas before their time, release
the heat that just might have been enough
to warm whole colonies of thoughtful people,
had they not been so untamed. But here at night—
when dangers all around make sleep an improbability
and no dawn can be counted on for any more than
the continual prolonging of everyone's ennui—
for all their ephemeral flickers, these flames
will have to do for sustenance, no further
fuller furnace for the spirit being available
under such rank conditions.
                              Let's be practical,
avoid becoming obsessed with the larger problem,
which is "economic" and "real," and stay put until

things somehow change and we, whether indefinitely
or for the suspended interval, sleep well again,
though not even the impoverished welcome death
since whatever can be imagined can be celebrated
and what cannot be, like hunger or eternal bliss,
is as easy to shy away from as it is to dismiss.

THE SHAPE OF SADNESS

This sadness like an evergreen dying
keeps its common shape, as it turns brown
and brittle, biding its time. It will not lift.
It will not tear its roots from underground
nor drop its needled branches, hard and dry,
nor splinter from some woodsman's searing saw
clearing the forest. It has taken years
to settle; now its slow descent claims all.

You may not note the differences, at first—
it shades the same, the wrinkles on its bark
peel off as effortlessly, streaks of sap
still promise sweetness inside, the odd lark
who finds a place for nesting here rejoices.
Only, the shade may somehow seem less cool,
the bark less pliable, the sap not so clear,
the lark's shrill call less gentle, and then, cruel.

DEATH IN VARIOUS PARTS

I

Never have I had such a fascination before
with the ripe valleys and soft contours,
the protruding stumps, the mangled fields
gathered heavy after a long warm shower
across their surface, like prostrate moslems
worshipping in small clumps, the breathing,
the brown motes huddled but distinct, the wet
new smell and aura of the glistening salt

of my own body. I am thirty-two years old
and this America that loves its health
tells me how now is my big chance: 1985.
The moon strains toward its second quarter
while somewhere else a starving man cries
out loud: "Bring us just one more harvest,
one more dish of the white stuff," dust
rising into the air above us both, muted.

My father—flagging, moneyed, stooped—
is dying of cancer, his fleshy stomach
criss-crossed by the purple profit graph
that guides the radioactive fire slicing
into him daily, like a damescene razor
riven into a bowl of rainbow pudding; his
hair is disappearing, white straw blown across
a desert, as I let my beard grow and high

above the abundant sand of the Sudan
a screeching horde of helicopters
holler their logical reply: "Help is
on the way, and nothing you can do will
stop it." I am feeling so clean now that love
needs only a lifted leg over me, a machine
that radiates from above, a goodwill feeding,
the certainty that nothing I do will stop it.

II

This is my death: the cigarette
I balance between my lips, this
bed, the open book beside it
I refuse to read, the words
inside it rising around me, my
blankets and the heat
I generate between my legs,
the missile keyed on me
outside Moscow somewhere,
hunger, this poem, the calendar
beyond the door there, the food
I ingested slowly last night,
the things she said to me,
the rash inside my thighs, that
severe fire, music I can't
listen to or will never
listen to, long warm showers,
styrofoam coffee, the river
churning against its own banks,
money, letters written, letters
never received, cold, naked
limbs, the word *there*, false
gods and water on the brain,
the kindness behind me, its
independent flicker, gas,
a dry throat, split hairs,
the long agony of sleep,
my boredom and astringent
fears, toppled bricks on my back
porch, green flagons of wine,
a broken cheer, his sudden
whistle, her recalled laughter,
your sweet coming to me

to be more sensitive
than clear, eyes glaring,
angels grouped in pairs,
a lone heron, yet another
more astounding but sudden
hope that someone, were that
someone not obliterated, too,
might be hearing this and care.

III

Since death is always extreme
why should it not begin
as far from me as the corner
of my big toe, a foreign
force of insurgents gathering
at the border of a rich and powerful
nation, i.e. me, to demonstrate
their cause for universal entropy
and pandemic peace for the living
inside—blood, cell, nerve, muscle?
Like a megalomaniac, my mind
rages that such a collection
of pains can bring me, finally,
to my weak knees, to dispatch
a thin index finger, scooping out
the problem there. This is just
the beginning. Later all morsels
of well-being, happiness in the state
of my body (genitals, teeth) will
collapse, next the cancer

will eat away at the very fabric,
white blood cells will overreact
with vigilante enthusiasm, form
wandering, heroic cults to stamp
out the evil, spreading through
the interior, and my aspirin, agents
of that ruling class, the gray matter
in the cold north, will travel
to every outback—ankle, elbow, arth-
ritic joint—subduing subversion
in those green provinces where once
a garden flourished, where pleasure,
the pleasure of small sailboats on
the open sea, eased its way
from the light, hairy forests
of my chest into the denser
tropics of the pelvic region,
the truly banana republic
I am,
      but the last to go,
and not without a struggle,
will be the bleeding heart
of the country whose tough strands
believe, believe in a life
yet to come, believe in the pulse
of their own nature, believe
the complexion of their fathers
must be carried on, cannot not be
carried on, while my flagging tongue,
the artists and the singers, who know
the heart, will pant, paint, and
proclaim their elevated love of
this native habitat, in groans,

in growls, in occasional elegies,
in the long agony of their sleep, as
now in their youth, in that garden
of their own making and majesty,
they look down on my infected toe,
the steady anguish of a few
agitations, and they mock it
in its ignorance of them, then turn
to the beauties of foreign
or virgin soils, lamenting their own
demise, yet yearning as never before
to become a part of someone else.

What It's Like To Travel Long Distance Alone On The Train

in memory of Addison H. Gery (1923-1985)

There's the sitting, quietly. And something else—
the long, vague expectation of a rising
like a great blue heron from some green marsh cove
another fifty miles or so down track
to get a drink of water. There're the lights
from unfamiliar spots you recognize,
those landmarks two more blocks or two more towns
from where you start anticipating them.
And passengers, the restless ones, wend by
imagining by walking backwards they,
in quantum leaps, will outwit time. They glance
at you, as you in glancing out the window
imagine who it is they think you are,
how little or how much they make of your
impassive stare, the title of the book
it seems you've just looked up from, as though words
when read on trains take longer to digress from,
or the distance from your point of origin
(some indeterminate shore in the past)
to where you're headed, near to, but beyond,
the place you really mean to go. There's sleep,
a public sleep you dip into and out of
with gull-like ease, in skittering ascent,
until your slackened body's not enough
to hold your private thoughts, and with it dreams
of perfect stillness, propped upright, the calm
of evenings when deep in an easy chair
your every nerve accepts the air. You will

each moment, smell each mile. You count each stop,
how many stops there'll be before your stop:
Eight, seven, six, five, four.... There's not much more,
except, of course, the landscapes, cities, dumps,
damp stations filled with waving families
and friends, unknown to you but intimate,
their every tear, once you regain full speed
in your uncertain journey toward the sun,
infecting your slow thought with sudden care
for what you know you'll never have again.
And as you turn from them and watch the sky,
you whisper to yourself, *good-bye! good-bye!*

SPEECH FOR A POSSIBLE ENDING

I don't know how things came to be
but their disintegration will
be witnessed, much as from the start
they offered hospitality
and even, later on, a thrill
or two for those who put the cart

before the horse and let it push:
We have surprises still. We fall
once we are old enough to know
better, we hear our footsteps crush
each idealistic principle
dropping onto our path like snow,

we watch our friends die, we enlist
the hours of darkness to supply
our equilibrium—that fails—
so when the anti-matter mist
devours our universe, nearby
the seasoned ones will shed their veils

to get a better look, and think,
if thinking is their way to act,
how little we were grateful for
those interruptions in the blink
of time we had, and how we lacked
the grace to know what to ignore.

MAKING YOUR WAY: AN EPITHALAMION

for Aline & Paul

You wonder again, *Is this the way they said it is?*
and the feeling you were supposed to be filled with
seems strangely behind you, a favorite bend
in the meandering toward a distinct future
you somehow missed, while the two of you—
one with an odd, dark smile, the other wearing a vest—
were happily singing some happy, dopey song
or just thinking your own pacific thoughts, each
folding into the other before it, the bushes, the hills,
shallow rivulets, scenes you'd frankly rather not
separate into their primary components, blending
with the syncopated pulses of thunder after lightning,
of the leafless trees you've come to expect in autumn,
of early darkness, of the gray sky carrying its snow.
But before you departed, this morning, from your dream
of this progress, this comfortable journey, you knew
exactly how that bend might appear to you, later,
like the welcome embrace of your loved ones
upon your arrival, its particular textures, soft
scent of pine, needled undergrowth, as familiar to you
as a voice or music.
                        You awoke from all this, refreshed.
How the turn was finally negotiated, what scant
copse escaped your attention, your wide eyes
wrapped in the breath of your mild companion,
matters little, once you are out in the open.
There is no savoring invisible things, not here, not
by conscious desire. Yet somehow the airy rightness
of travel, the hum of the one next to you, radiance
you can't see, could never see, wavering
above the horizon behind you, the glow which guides

and follows, guides and follows, now spills over
like water into your hands, like tears onto your cheeks,
and you sense together the two of you have been there,
all of us have been there, or will have been there
at one time or another, just passing through, maybe,
singing or otherwise. And we shall speak of this often,
throwing our arms around each other, the several branches
of one family, as we wave you off on your own way.

23 August 1987

JOHN GERY is from Lititz, Pennsylvania, and attended Princeton, the University of Chicago, and Stanford, where he was a Mirrielees Fellow in Creative Writing. His previous books include *Charlemagne: A Song of Gestures* (1983), *The Burning of New Orleans* (1988), and *Three Poems* (1989), and his critical work *Nuclear Annihilation and Contemporary American Poetry: Ways of Nothingness* is forthcoming from the University Press of Florida. An Associate Professor of English at the University of New Orleans, he has also taught literature and creative writing at Stanford, San Jose State, and the University of Iowa, as well as at Brunnenburg Castle, Italy. He has received an NEA Fellowship, the Deep South Writers Poetry Award, and the Academy of American Poets Prize, among other awards.